After Eden

Roberta Senechal de la Roche

The Heartland Review Press/Elizabethtown, KY

Copyright©2018 Roberta Senechal de la Roche
All rights reserved

This book may not be reproduced, in whole or in part, including illustrations, in any form (beyond that copying permitted by Section 107 and 108 of the US Copyright Law and except by reviewers for the public press), without written permission from the publisher.

Printed in the USA

ISBN 978-0-9996868-4-3
$12.95

Cover art: *Lone Soldier* by Lucinda Wride

Printed by Ingram-Spark

ACKNOWLEDGEMENTS

Black Fox Literary Magazine, "After Ophelia"

Cold Creek Review, "Lost"

Orange Review, "Metamorphosis"

I-70 Review, "Divertimento," "Minor Key," "Moving Parts," and "Savage Weeds"

Vallum, "After Eden,"

Table of Contents

Moving Parts	6
Metamorphosis	7
After Eden	8
Lost	9
Divertimento	10
Autumn Light	11
Blue Mountain	12
Minor Key	13
Burning Violins	14
Savage Weeds	15
Bottle of Sleep	16
The Sound of Blue	17
Side Effect	18
The Crow Poem	19
Nor'easter	20
After Ophelia	21
Behind Her Lipstick	22
The Red Shoes	23
White Room	24
Frost Tattoo	25

AFTER EDEN

Moving Parts

Mother said if you want to walk straight,
do not look down or up.
She did not say memory
can melt like wax in a house fire
or that cretaceous glaciers long since
scoured away ancestral naked footsteps.

She did not say you must find your way
through whirling steel or dust or bad music,
over bridges falling down, but only said
Forget: make it your favorite verb,
then disappeared through a blue door
at the top of a high staircase.

We ride in on slow somnolent tides,
turn the music up, raise our cups and sing:

Graffiti texts on harbor walls imply
that they who come on ships will oxidize
if they ever settle down

as though it was a light matter, as though
we would always keep
moving, never really come to shore.

At sea, we never touched the heart of oaks
or met the owl's feral stare
or saw borders lit with flaming swords
or heard earth's teeth grit, waiting to grind us
into dark and primal loam to give
its yearning grass its due.

Everything comes back to spill the glass
one way or another, she said.
She did not say it might be worth it
to turn our bow into the gale, leaning into high
unfurling waves, singing into the mouth of fog,
embracing all the moving forms of endless blue.

Metamorphosis

When the world gets small and tight, we want
someone who goes too far
when no one else will even try to mime
the dying art of fire,

someone who can talk to rain
the way the rain can talk to grass:

>   Come up
>   and make it green again,

who can speak from a tree
without ever leaning on a branch,
weightless almost,
even when no one else listens.

Take all the breath of candles
where the elders sinned,
all the chairs they could not fill
and put them in the wind,

Gather scars as though we own them,
tear down the scaffolding of our past, lean
into animate light that will pull us up
like plants out of the savage ground.

After Eden

It's not for me to specify
what part of this is choreographed or real.
Only children say the moon breathes deep
as it goes to ground at night
watched by angels holding roses,
by an owl nodding obsessively
on a singular branch.

I think it's better if we never know
how difficult it is to get things started
when even in the best of times
the light flickers on and off,
when nature always spends so much
that it takes all we have to ignore
the hard life of sparrows in the streets.

It's not for me to say what happened after Eden.
I just watch you breathe your innocence at night,
almost unbroken by shadows, almost childlike.

We say we want these things again:
small birds who speak to us, unafraid
large trees that gently lean to shade us,
although we know we can't turn back
the winter's claim on spring, on roses,
on strangers solitary on their way.

Lost

You were born wrong, too soon
or something like combustion or flood.
Original hands caressed to hate
what little you had left.

Once you rolled that stone,
it was too late to bite the tongue
to split all the words.

Worlds of circles followed,
and filled with dust.

Divertimento

Maybe it starts when you grow thin on irony,
find you can no longer bring into focus
naked empty branches
moving fast outside your window.
Since the thrushes are all flown,
winter seems all too literal.

Maybe piano music goes
best with this moment,
or slow violins in a minor key,
or unconjugated verbs expressed
by all known birds gone off, away
when the temperature starts falling fast.

What if I put parakeets and tinsel in my rooms,
turn up the heat only to see
frost cut stencils on my panes,
as light leans down along its dark couch,
as mountains empty out their eastern face?

Could we pretend we are still going
through the channel, hauling
deep until we sound, then pulling hard
for shore and windward
where we would lift a cup or two?

For lack of somewhere else to go,
I hold myself with both arms, tight
against unspoken words,
and those not taken back,
open only to the cold.

Autumn Light

It's how the weather comes
sometimes, especially
when you're not looking
that makes you feel it more.

A lower arc of sun, perhaps
you hear the evening sparrows
high in naked boughs inquire
Is it time to go?

Twilight seems so early now,
But why the table laid with white,
the empty glass beside the plate
without a knife?

Blue Mountain

When I last heard your steps
on the blue mountain, mist was
raveled gray silk slipping
down its metamorphic face,
sifting through dark stands of pine.

Up where sky has no doors or bars
you looked back from the high edge,
leaning on a weathered tree
pretending to court danger,
unwinded though, still unbent.

Going down was easier
though the footing was less sure
over old moraines, through lowering light
gold touching only treetops
so late in the day.

>A black stream below
>where one imagines Dante
>on his haunches weeping in the dark
>rising, two lovers in the burning
>wind mounting to eternal gyre.

Just as your back becomes a shadow arch
rising with my fingers, immanent, ready to go
free falling anywhere that wayward night
might chance, hanging on each other's words,
we find that we are lost.

Now exhale everything that reason, wind, or entropy
can nullify; accept as grace the swallow's wing,
the waning crescent as your talisman, unrepentant
through the deep and sleeping woods, take flight
before some change can make us strange or still.

Minor Key

We love this world too much
to escape it by ourselves, alone
like a rabbit in a tightening snare, deceived
mistaking surfaces for substance, not seeing
that city lights unstar the sky at night,
that time can slack all fine tuned guitars.

Just remember as the last wild geese recede
from your field of vision, what you can't take
but won't let go, though you are finished
with difficult landscapes scattered
with small illusions and cheap memorials
lit by electric trees.

Remember as prodigal weeds come breach your dooryard,
as starlings come to perch along the windowsills,
inscrutable in their high tonguing
but telling us the time, though we can no longer sing,
we still can pantomime our innocence to them
in hopes of hearing rising wings.

Burning Violins

The rose has the advantage of thorns,
but we arrive naked, disarmed
with all our words in present tense.

Moths have no theory of the light,
but rise unthinking
toward all attractive flames.

You make it up as you go, invisible
means to ends, only to find
blind heat and stumbling angels.

So you take up your burning violins,
cultivate the fire arts, go tango fast enough
and leave your fortune to the wind.

Savage Weeds

Is it wrong to love this world
with its metal tongue and heart of fire
inflaming sunsets over summer roads
where trees throw down their shaking shadows
to the slow rise and fall
of sweet cicada singsong through the air?

Though we do not have wings
and have been handed machines instead of lilies,
we know the score, that it is not
just meter, pitch, or feel or tempo,
but anything with rain in the background,
anything that's touched by light.

Should we renounce the names of stars
because we learn they are only
whirling stones and cold,
or the swallows who draw the eye
because they are only hurtling sacks of blood
strung out on hollow bone?

Still we save our cherished pebbles
smoothed by tides, although
it makes no sense to name the things
we take in hand, as savage weeds
will cover all. But going out, we still
will covet all the glowing goldenrod,
the silver yarrow, the scent of thyme.

Bottle of Sleep

I tried to carry your bottle of sleep,
watching as you said too much
at last call, as the lights went down
as the barkeep rang it up
and you did not want
to go back home.

Devil's got bad teeth, they say,
a crooked mind, but a way
with the ladies, smooth enough
so we can sing along
through the usual burning
we earn in time.

If it was dawn in the temple,
would you still give me
those mourning hands coming up
and under, tear the veil
you said you swore by
though others surely came before?

What does it take
to make us speak in magnolia
tongues again, into sweet gum skies
with honeysuckled breath,
our feet on tender grass,
the patient worm below?

Let us now recall the sound of snow,
of glaciers spreading slow blue hands
of leviathan calling in the quiet deep,
the significance of clouds, of rain,
of what we had before the ripening
of fatal fruit, our sugared gain.

The Sound of Blue

On seeing beautiful hands draw away,
though wanting everything
three pearls, grey eyes, red silk, or grace,
you learn soon enough
you cannot bargain with silence,
however transcendent it might seem at first.

They say a string must be pulled tight
to make it sonorous when struck.
Sorrow can do this too, sounds
just as good when plucked softly
in a minor key after midnight,
when no one else can hear.

Our veins are open now, so
we can return to the sea, where
petrels come down and bless our sinking
faces, brush the chaos from our eyes
with a single feather, give us the sound of blue,
of depth, eternal roll of waves.

Side Effect

Try not to forget
how it goes up
what all the burning is for

Even as our best chagrin goes cold
as we follow rivers broken by stones,
by the weight of cities sick with night

on a dark planet turning
with or without us, a scuffed shoe here,
hollow bone there, a faint and muffled bell.

Is it less than the drowning
we thought we wanted
in the first place,

something soft and mordant
ripened in some corner after midnight
in a dim century?

Here is a flower for us all, heart red,
and something more than breath
than dancing, leaning into waltz

into fungus dread all white,
into the dark the deep the sweet
beloved damned night

over the tent we cannot raise again:
body to the dark, soul to the light
voice into mouths of birds.

The Crow Poem

Crows follow behind the summer haying,
stepping and bowing with their slow
deliberate corvid grace.

The blade is kind to them, yielding red
gleanings from small violence in the grass.
Not so with us,

we who try to turn aside the stroke
that ends with sounding raptor wings
praise-singing us into shadow.

In the sweat of our brow we rush
to gather in our gain, ignoring dark flocks
that rise to race the coming storm.

Nor'easter

Do not say I wanted to lie with you
just to make an end of journeys,
to make a wave.
I could always swim to land, alone.

I could take everything you lost and more
but we have so little time to find
a transept in this storm,
what kinds of things it casts ashore,

And at landfall we must walk the dunes,
blink spindrift from our eyes
while the juggler on his dark horse behind
keeps to a polite distance,

Then put on our feather masks
and fire dance before him
while books of luminescence slowly close,
as northering sky runs out of breath.

After Ophelia

Anyone who cared to look
could see the bridge was on fire,
especially at night.

We'd gone over it, back and forth
a long time, while I put upon my lips
the way of sourwood blossoms

where a choleric wolf used to cross
where a brindled owl looked for its chance
where we once watched water pass below.

Naming these always makes it worse
and doesn't help any floating thing
waiting to go under and forget.

Behind Her Lipstick

A bad start and the middle not so great, so
If you have the chance, leave
the last door locked, in case
something comes around again,
though you know I don't believe.

Absent, turning cup then wedding ring,
speaking, her hands rise and fall,
tired doves settling, Jesus,
settling.

Across a burning table
through cold space, she says
my skin is frost,
your name is smoke
gets in your eyes, you shall be fire,
combustible.
My name means
born by accident
I will be ash.

Gates of flesh closing
losing edge, unmade sense
going out in circles, generations'
secrets clench behind her lipstick,
red, still perfectly applied,
and pursed,

saving face. Ebony eyes set in dark ivory,
hermetic beneath roiling curls,
withholding, not bequeathing
true colors, names, or place of birth, Lord,
not even place.

The Red Shoes

Light does not escape
from this.

I wear my dead
mother's little shoes
red patent leather, gilt
buckles, audacious
heels pristine,
intact.

When I look down
she is here again
just now, elegant
in winter's crystal rooms,
program clenched
in black-gloved hands,
impeccable
someone at her elbow,
transparent, guiding her
to a door that opens up
behind the stage.

Light does not escape from her
closet full of shoes,
like an opaque rainbow
in the dark, waiting
for someone else to dance.

White Room

Everything we touch turns back
to what it was before it had a shape,
but there is no getting over
when we first loved.

More than exhalation in a room
all white, or sunset moving down
your face, more
than echoes coming back
out of far blue valleys.

There is no getting out of it,
when heat escapes by night, so cold
small birds freeze and fall
from branches into snow.

We know when frost gives way
to green, the inevitable,
that we are supposed to say
that being empty can make us full,
that being gone
can make us warm.

Frost Tattoo

And does it open to you,
this gray sky, its wind
churning from northeast
through ranks of oak
breaking ground with splintered frost,
spears of sleet, arctic scattershot
affliction sown in frozen fields?

Cold burns as well as heat, he said
at last putting on a heavy coat, door shut
hard woods now black and clean and spare
calligraphy
sketched on what is new and white
and shining out a memory of sun.

Things fall away from us,
a rose tattoo that once drew blood,
songs under paper moons, backlit
the color red, the heated spoons, your fret
worn guitar in my hands, the tune
you could not carry, the passing out,
intemperate sights.

Let us now lie down deep within this storm
like a clench of chrysalis green inside
beneath a sleeping branch, waiting,
hypothermic
for wild geese sounding north.
If anyone, they should know when it is time
to leave and when to let go
our talismans of words as we rise
up and into vernal light.

www.ingramcontent.com/pod-product-compliance
Lightning Source LLC
Chambersburg PA
CBHW070443010526
44118CB00014B/2175